Entrepreneurial Freedom

*How to Start and Grow
A Profitable Virtual Assistance Practice*

Companion Workbook

2nd Edition

by
Jeannine Clontz and Lauren Hidden

For information please contact:
Biz-E Press
Jeannine Clontz
636-282-9660
Jeannine@Accbizsvcs.com

Entrepreneurial Freedom: *How to Start and*
Grow A Profitable Virtual Assistance Practice
Companion Workbook, 2nd Edition
Edited by: Lauren Hidden
Layout by: Jeannine Clontz
Cover Design by: Studio H
Published by: Biz-E Press
Printed in the U.S.A. by: CreateSpace.com

Publisher's Cataloging-in-Publication
(Provided by Quality Books, Inc.)

Clontz, Jeannine.
    Entrepreneurial freedom : *how to start and grow a*
    profitable virtual assistance practice : companion
    workbook / by Jeannine Clontz and Lauren Hidden - 2nd ed..
        p. cm.
        ISBN-13: 978-0-9785941-4-5
        ISBN-10: 0-9785941-4-2

    1. Administrative assistants–Problems, exercises,
    etc. 2. Virtual reality in management–Problems,
    exercises, etc. 3. Home-based businesses–Problems,
    exercises, etc. 4. New business enterprises–Problems,
    exercises, etc.   I. Hidden, Lauren. II. Title.

HF5547.5.C581 2011   651.3'068'1
                        QBI10-600225

Library of Congress Control Number: 2010917454

Chapter One: Do You Have What it Takes

What you need to get started:

Capital

I believe I will need $ _____ working capital to start my business.

I currently have $ _____ , the balance will be obtained from:

___ home refinance	___ credit card
___ home equity line	___ sale of personal property/collectibles
___ loan from friends/family	___ SBA loan
___ personal loan w/collateral	___ investor financing
___ business loan	

Funding source detail: _____

Total amount borrowed: $ _____   Interest rate: _____%

Monthly payment obligation: $ _____

Retail Space?   ___ Yes ___ No

Square footage needed: _____   Average cost/square foot: $ _____

Retail space actual cost: $ _____/month

What's Your Experience?

Briefly describe your skill-set as it relates to the business products/services you'll provide:

_____

_____

_____

What corporate or business related skills do you have to assist you in starting your business?

_____

_____

_____

How will I persevere?

What time/effort can I devote to building:

A Network:_____

_____

_____

My self-confidence & being comfortable in getting out there and promoting my business:

_____

_____

_____

Summary

What resources have been helpful and/or what additional information do I need to investigate in order to 'have what it takes' to start my business?

_____

_____

_____

_____

_____

Chapter Two: Planning Your Business

I plan to start my business: ___ **Part-time**   ___ **Full-time**

If starting part-time, I plan to take my business full-time by: _____

date or time period

Setting up your office: (use Start-up Options on Page 34 to add costs)

Business phone equipment   ___ have $ _____ to purchase

Business phone service $ _____ monthly

Computer   ___ have $ _____ to purchase

Software   ___ have $ _____ to purchase

Additional software needs/updates for first year $ _____ to purchase

Scanner   ___ no need   ___ have $ _____ to purchase

Copier   ___ no need   ___ have $ _____ to purchase

Transcription   ___ no need   ___ have $ _____ to purchase

Bookkeeping Software   ___ have $ _____ to purchase

Fax Machine   ___ have $ _____ to purchase

Office Rent   ___ no need   ___ have $ _____ monthly

Office supplies   ___ have $ _____ to purchase/
                                                                                                           monthly

Printer (laserjet)   ___ have $ _____ to purchase

Printer (color or inkjet)   ___ have $ _____ to purchase

Answering machine   ___ have $ _____ to purchase

Calculator   ___ have $ _____ to purchase

Website development   ___ have $ _____ to start

Website hosting   ___ have $ _____ monthly

Marketing materials

Brochures   ___ have $ _____ to purchase

Letterhead   ___ have $ _____ to purchase

Business cards   ___ have $ _____ to purchase

Professional Membership Budget $ _____ first year

I plan to organize my company as:

___ Sole Proprietor   Cost: $ _____

___ Partnership or LLC   Cost: $ _____

___ Corporation   Cost: $ _____

Business Plan

___ I have set up and will maintain my own business plan

___ I have all the necessary data and will hire someone to develop my plan

Cost: $ _____

Contracts and Forms

For my particular business I will need:

___ Work for Hire Agreement

___ Specialty Client Agreement based on my Niche

___ Sub-contractor Agreement

___ Retainer Agreement

___ Time Record

___ Resume Questionnaire

___ Telephone Contact Sheets

___ Other _____

___ Other _____

Record Keeping

I am using _____ to keep track of my business expenses and receipts, client invoicing, etc.

Other record keeping options I'm considering:_____

Delegating Business Tasks

If applicable, I need:

___ CPA   My CPA is: _____

___ attorney   My attorney is: _____

___ insurance   My insurance agent is:_____

___ other   My _____

___ other   My _____

Taking into consideration all of the planning outlined above, my initial getting started

budget is: $ _____

My on-going monthly budget is: $ _____

My annual budget will be: $ _____

I will need to generate $ _____ per month in sales and profit to maintain this

budget.

Summary

What resources have been helpful and/or what additional information do I need to
investigate in order to plan my business?

_____

_____

_____

_____

_____

Chapter Three: Branding

Business Name

My top three business names are:

1. _____

2. _____

3. _____

My business will be named: _____

Taglines

Consider three options for taglines—they may be used in different situations

1. _____

2. _____

3. _____

My main tagline will be: _____

30-second infomercial (elevator speech)

_____

_____

_____

_____

_____

_____

Creating a Website

My website will need the following pages:

____ About us content should include: _____

_____

_____

____ Products/services content to include: _____

_____

_____

____ Links/resources to include: _____

_____

_____

____ Contact us content to include: _____

_____

____ Sample work to include: _____

_____

_____

____ Testimonial to include: _____

_____

____ Articles/Press to include: _____

_____

_____

____ Pricing to include: _____

_____

Creating a Website (continued)

____ Other to include: _____

_____

____ Other to include: _____

_____

Going Live

____ Domain name _____

____ Domain name registered   Cost $ _____ per month – per year

____ Hosting by: Cost $ _____ per month – per year

____ Doing it myself

____ Hiring: _____   Cost $ _____ per month – per year

Once 'live', view it in a variety of browsers to make sure you are pleased with the look and feel:

___ Internet Explorer   ___ AOL   ___ Yahoo   ___ Firefox   ___ Other

Keywords and Metatags

I will use the following keywords/metatags on my website (what words might someone put into a search engine if they were seeking your type of service?) – Include your company name, several variations of 'virtual assistant' or VA, i.e., real estate virtual assistant (niche), graphic design VA, etc.

_____

_____

_____

_____

_____

E-mail Signature Lines

My signature line will include: ___ Web URL   ___ Tagline   ___ Newsletter sign-up

___ Other sign-up links   ___ Certification designations

___ Phone/fax/e-mail contact info   ___ Company name/logos   ___ Brief benefits list

___ List of new services   ___ membership in an industry association

___ announce upcoming seminars/trainings

My signature line will be: _____

_____

_____

_____

_____

Setting Your Rates

My rates will be based on the following:

Income goal $ _____ per year

Hours per week to perform client projects: _____ hours

Divide income goal by 12 (months); then 4 (weeks); then by number of hours per week to establish your base hourly rate of: $ _____

On-going expenses amount to: $ _____ per month.
Divide this amount by 12 (months); then 4 (weeks) then by the number of hours per week to established your base hourly rate of: $ _____

I will add the following profit margin of $ _____ per hour to my rate to set aside to grow and expand my business.

My hourly rate is: $ _____

This will be the rate used for basic services.

Setting Your Rates (continued)

Based on the additional expertise required to perform other duties, my rates will be:

Service: _____ Rate: $ _____

Service: _____ Rate: $ _____

Service: _____ Rate: $ _____

Service: _____ Rate: $ _____

Service: _____ Rate: $ _____

Service: _____ Rate: $ _____

Service: _____ Rate: $ _____

Service: _____ Rate: $ _____

Service: _____ Rate: $ _____

Service: _____ Rate: $ _____

Service: _____ Rate: $ _____

Packages and Programs

My _____ Package/Program will include:

_____

_____

_____

Package/Program Cost: $ _____

My _____ Package/Program will include:

_____

_____

_____

Package/Program Cost: $ _____

Packages and Programs (continued)

My _____ Package/Program will include:

_____

_____

_____

Package/Program Cost: $ _____

My _____ Package/Program will include:

_____

_____

_____

Package/Program Cost: $ _____

Setting Client Criteria

"A" Clients will meet the following criteria: _____

_____

_____

_____

"B" Clients will meet the following criteria: _____

_____

_____

_____

"C" Clients will meet the following criteria: _____

_____

_____

_____

Ideal Client Profile

My ideal client has the following characteristics:

_____

_____

_____

_____

_____

Tracking Time on Task

Tracking client project time will be done using the following method: _____

_____

Professional Image

I will incorporate these additional considerations into developing my professional image:

____ professional 'business' attire

____ professional haircut

____ professional accessories (grooming and/or business equipment)

____ open and confident body language

____ speaking in a friendly tone with an appropriate level of volume

____ forms and marketing materials (brochure, letterhead, business cards)

____ company logo

____ positive attitude about my company's status and my competitors'

____ refusal to discuss or name particular clients or their business practices

____ be professional 24/7 and look and feel like a business owner

Summary

What resources have I found helpful and/or what additional information do I need to investigate in order to finalize my branding?

_____

_____

_____

_____

_____

_____

_____

Chapter Four: How to Find and Keep Clients

Networking Groups

I will commit to being involved with (#) _____ networking groups. At least (#) _____ will be local, and (#) _____ will be Internet based. The networking groups I am researching and considering are:

1. _____   Cost $ _____   ___ Yes ___ No

2. _____   Cost $ _____   ___ Yes ___ No

3. _____   Cost $ _____   ___ Yes ___ No

4. _____   Cost $ _____   ___ Yes ___ No

5. _____   Cost $ _____   ___ Yes ___ No

6. _____   Cost $ _____   ___ Yes ___ No

7. _____   Cost $ _____   ___ Yes ___ No

I plan to build my network in the following ways:

_____

_____

_____

Social Media Marketing Networks I will join:

___ Twitter   ___ Facebook   ___ LinkedIn   _____ Other

_____ Other   _____ Other   _____ Other

I plan to build my network in the following ways:

_____

_____

_____

Taking my network to the next level will include being a speaker and/or writing articles. My options for speaking topics could include:

_____   _____

_____   _____

Options for article topics could include:

_____   _____

_____   _____

Ways I could market myself as a speaker include:

_____   _____

_____   _____

Places to submit articles include:

_____   _____

_____   _____

_____   _____

Overcoming Client Objections:

I will overcome client objections on the subjects below by:

Pricing:_____

_____

Working off-site: _____

_____

Turnaround time: _____

_____

Communicating with Clients:

Most client projects will be communicated by:

___ E-mail   ___ Fax   ___ Snail mail   ___ Voice recording   ___ Diskette or CD

___ Online file sharing   ___ GotomyPC, PCanywhere or like software

Outline client instructions for communicating projects and communicating during the project as issues arise:

_____

_____

_____

Handling Difficult Clients

How I can analyze whether this client is having issues with the virtual nature of my business or is truly a 'difficult' client I should walk away from?

_____

_____

_____

What exit strategy I will use if I need to sever a client relationship?

_____

_____

_____

Local Businesses Versus Virtual Clients

My local area is a viable business option ___ Yes ___ No (more rural)

Research your local market to decide whether or not you should invest your marketing dollars on local connections. Local research information includes:

_____

_____

_____

_____

What additional time might be required to service local clients?_____

_____

_____

What additional expenses will be incurred serving local clients? _____

_____

_____

What volunteer opportunities might be necessary to connect with local clients?

_____

_____

Based on the above information, I believe most of my business will be:

___ Local   ___ Internet based

Most of my marketing dollars should be used to market to potential clients that are:

___ Local   ___ Internet based

What percentage of my marketing budget will be spent on marketing to clients that are:

Local _____ %   Internet based _____%

Ethics and Customer Service

How I will communicate (in print and online) that I maintain the highest levels of ethics and customer service:

_____

_____

_____

My customer service pledge will be: _____

_____

_____

_____

I will update this pledge _____ times a year.

I will continue to improve my customer service skills by:

   ___ Reading books   ___ Taking online or local classes

   ___ Reading online articles and/or blogs

   ___ Other: _____

I will use my customer service pledge in the following manner:

   ___ Brochure   ___ Website   ___ Infomercial   ___ Branding

   ___ Other: _____

Saying "No" to a Potential Client

As I build my network, I will become the resource for potential clients that don't fit my expertise. Until my network grows, and/or if a potential client doesn't fit my expertise, I will use the following options to say "no", while still helping the potential client to find a solution:

_____

_____

_____

_____

_____

_____

Firing Clients

I will 'fire' clients in a way to allow them to feel enriched by the experience and maintain a high regard for the VA industry. My professional way to handle firing a client will include:

_____

_____

_____

_____

Collections

My options for collections include:

___ Detail in my client contract what the payment options/expectations are

___ Require 50% up-front

___ Require final 50% payment before returning project

___ Offer discount for paying in a certain number of days

___ Work on retainer

___ Other: _____

Once payment is past due, I will initiate the following process in collections:

_____

_____

_____

_____

Collections (continued)

If my collections process does not result in payment, I will consider writing off debt

for volume of $ _____ or less, and secure a collections service to handle debt

of $ _____ or more.

Collections service options include: _____

_____

Summary

What resources have been helpful and/or what additional information do I need to investigate in order to find and keep clients?:

_____

_____

_____

_____

_____

_____

_____

Chapter Five: Professional Development

Continuing Education

What options for continuing education will be needed and where will I go to learn them?

Update software skills: _____

_____

_____

Business skills: _____

_____

_____

Internet industry and business trends: _____

_____

_____

New technologies: _____

_____

_____

Industry and Small Business Conferences

I will add $ _____ to my annual budget to attend industry/business conferences.

Research indicates the following as viable options for my type of virtual assistance practice:

Event held by: _____

Conference cost: $ _____

Approximate airfare/hotel costs: $ _____

Meals not included with registration: $ _____

Why this event is important to my professional development: _____

_____

_____

Event held by: _____

Conference cost: $ _____

Approximate airfare/hotel costs: $ _____

Meals not included with registration: $ _____

Why this event is important to my professional development: _____

_____

_____

Event held by: _____

Conference cost: $ _____

Approximate airfare/hotel costs: $ _____

Meals not included with registration: $ _____

Why this event is important to my professional development: _____

_____

_____

Event held by: _____

Conference cost: $ _____

Approximate airfare/hotel costs: $ _____

Meals not included with registration: $ _____

Why this event is important to my professional development: _____

_____

_____

Certifications

Research indicates the following certifications would be helpful in developing my type of virtual assistance practice:

I will add $ _____ to my annual budget for certifications

Certification offered by: _____

Cost $ _____

Time required for testing: _____

____ Online   ____ On-site

Are classes/training offered or required prior to testing?:   ____ Yes   ____ No

Time required for training: _____

Are study guides provided?   ____ Yes   ____ No

Is recertification required at any time?   ____ Yes   ____ No

Why this certification is important to my professional development: _____

_____

_____

Certification offered by: _____

Cost $ _____

Time required for testing: _____

____ Online   ____ On-site

Are classes/training offered or required prior to testing?:   ____ Yes   ____ No

Time required for training: _____

Are study guides provided?   ____ Yes   ____ No

Is recertification required at any time?   ____ Yes   ____ No

Why this certification is important to my professional development: _____

_____

_____

Certification offered by: _____

Cost $ _____

Time required for testing: _____

____ Online   ____ On-site

Are classes/training offered or required prior to testing?   ____ Yes   ____ No

Time required for training: _____

Are study guides provided?:   ____ Yes   ____ No

Is recertification required at any time?   ____ Yes   ____ No

Why this certification is important to my professional development: _____

_____

_____

Certification offered by: _____

Cost $ _____

Time required for testing: _____

____ Online   ____ On-site

Are classes/training offered or required prior to testing?   ____ Yes   ____ No

Time required for training: _____

Are study guides provided?   ____ Yes   ____ No

Is recertification required at any time?   ____ Yes   ____ No

Why this certification is important to my professional development: _____

_____

_____

Professional Associations

I will add $ _____ to my annual budget for Professional Association Memberships.

I have found the following associations to be beneficial to my type of business:

Association: _____

___ Locally based   ___ Internet based   Membership Cost: $ _____

Volunteer options: _____

_____

Association: _____

___ Locally based   ___ Internet based   Membership Cost: $ _____

Volunteer options: _____

_____

Association: _____

___ Locally based   ___ Internet based   Membership Cost: $ _____

Volunteer options: _____

_____

Association: _____

___ Locally based   ___ Internet based   Membership Cost: $ _____

Volunteer options: _____

_____

Books

These are the books I will read to enhance my professional development:

_____

_____

_____

_____

The Web

The following are web-based sites that I have found beneficial to my professional development:

_____
Website URL

Type of information: _____

_____
Website URL

Type of information: _____

_____
Website URL

Type of information: _____

_____
Website URL

Type of information: _____

_____
Website URL

Type of information: _____

_____
Website URL

Type of information: _____

_____
Website URL

Type of information: _____

_____
Website URL

Type of information: _____

Podcasts

The following podcasts are beneficial to my professional development:

_____

Podcast URL

Type of information: _____

_____

Podcast URL

Type of information: _____

_____

Podcast URL

Type of information: _____

_____

Podcast URL

Type of information: _____

_____

Podcast URL

Type of information: _____

_____

Podcast URL

Type of information: _____

_____

Podcast URL

Type of information: _____

_____

Podcast URL

Type of information: _____

_____

Podcast URL

Type of information: _____

Blogs

The following blogs are beneficial to my professional development:

_____

Blog URL

Type of information: _____

_____

Blog URL

Type of information: _____

_____

Blog URL

Type of information: _____

_____

Blog URL

Type of information: _____

_____

Blog URL

Type of information: _____

_____

Blog URL

Type of information: _____

Summary

What resources have been helpful and/or what additional information do I need to investigate in order to enhance my professional development?

_____

_____

_____

_____

Chapter Six: Marketing, Advertising & Public Relations

Marketing

My marketing budget will be: $ _____ or _____% of my operating budget.

Paid Advertising

I will incorporate the following types of paid advertisement for my business:

___ Yellow Pages   ___ Trade magazines   ___ Radio/TV   ___ Internet based

Other: _____

_____

Bartering – Is this viable for my business: ____ Yes   ____ No

Options (don't forget to discuss with your CPA so you know your tax liabilities of this

option): _____

_____

_____

Tracking My Results

I will use the following options for tracking my marketing results:

_____

_____

_____

_____

Word of Mouth Marketing

I will implement the following practices in order to utilize word of mouth marketing:

Leads Groups to consider:

Group: _____   Membership Cost: $ _____

Meeting Cost: $ _____   How often do they meet?: _____

Size of Group: _____ ____ Online ____ Local

Advantages of joining this particular group: _____

_____

Group: _____ Membership Cost: $ _____

Meeting Cost: $ _____ How often do they meet? _____

Size of Group: _____ ____ Online ____ Local

Advantages of joining this particular group: _____

_____

Group: _____ Membership Cost: $ _____

Meeting Cost: $ _____ How often do they meet? _____

Size of Group: _____ ____ Online ____ Local

Advantages of joining this particular group: _____

_____

Group: _____ Membership Cost: $ _____

Meeting Cost: $ _____ How often do they meet? _____

Size of Group: _____ ____ Online ____ Local

Advantages of joining this particular group: _____

_____

Group: _____ Membership Cost: $ _____

Meeting Cost: $ _____ How often do they meet? _____

Size of Group: _____ ____ Online ____ Local

Advantages of joining this particular group: _____

_____

How to Get Free Publicity

I will utilize the following forms of free publicity: _____

_____

_____

_____

_____

Sales

I will incorporate the following questions in order to identify a potential client need:

_____

_____

_____

_____

_____

_____

_____

Questions I can ask to help them 'close' the sale:

_____

_____

_____

_____

_____

_____

_____

Giveaways

I will utilize the following promotional items or giveaways for my business:

_____

_____

_____

_____

Social Media Marketing

I will utilize the following social media platforms to promote and market my practice:

Platform (Blog.): _____

My Domain will be: _____

Hosted by: _____   Theme:_____

Login: _____   Password: _____

Additional Pages to include:

_____

_____

_____

_____

Focus blog postings on these topics:

_____

_____

_____

Time to devote each week: _____ hours

Platform (i.e. Twitter, etc.): _____

My URL for others to connect to me: _____

Login: _____   Password: _____

Profile elements to include: _____

Website/Blog URLs to promote:_____

Focus on which target groups:

_____

Time to devote each week: _____ hours

Platform (i.e. Twitter, etc.): _____

My URL for others to connect to me: _____

Login: _____   Password: _____

Profile elements to include: _____

Website/Blog URLs to promote:_____

Focus on which target groups:

_____

Time to devote each week: _____ hours

Platform (i.e. Twitter, etc.): _____

My URL for others to connect to me: _____

Login: _____   Password: _____

Profile elements to include: _____

Website/Blog URLs to promote:_____

Focus on which target groups:

_____

Time to devote each week: _____ hours

Platform (i.e. Twitter, etc.): _____

My URL for others to connect to me: _____

Login: _____   Password: _____

Profile elements to include: _____

Website/Blog URLs to promote:_____

Focus on which target groups:

_____

Time to devote each week: _____ hours

Bookmarking Sites

I will participate and connect blog postings to these bookmarking sites:

Site: _____

Login: _____   Password: _____

Types of posts to include:

_____

Site: _____

Login: _____   Password: _____

Types of posts to include:

_____

Site: _____

Login: _____   Password: _____

Types of posts to include:

_____

Site: _____

Login: _____ Password: _____

Types of posts to include:

_____

Audio/Video

Type of medium (i.e. audio or video): _____

Topics to use:

_____ _____ _____

Post to:

_____ _____ _____

Type of medium (i.e. audio or video): _____

Topics to use:

_____ _____ _____

Post to:

_____ _____ _____

Type of medium (i.e. audio or video): _____

Topics to use:

_____ _____ _____

Post to:

_____ _____ _____

Type of medium (i.e. audio or video): _____

Topics to use:

_____ _____ _____

Post to:

_____ _____ _____

Summary

What resources have I found helpful and/or what additional information do I need to investigate in order to finalize my marketing, branding and PR:

_____

_____

_____

_____

_____

_____

_____

_____

_____

_____

Chapter Seven: The Challenges of Working From Home

Balancing Work and Home

I will incorporate and balance work, play and home in the following way:

_____

_____

_____

_____

Scheduling and Boundaries

I will use the following system(s) to organize my professional schedule:

_____

_____

_____

I will use the following system(s) to organize my personal schedule:

_____

_____

_____

I will set boundaries with clients as follows:

_____

_____

I will set boundaries with family and friends as follows:

_____

_____

I will maintain good self-esteem and business management as follows:

_____

_____

_____

Handling Isolation

Select One:

___ Isolation is not an issue for me. (Skip to **Handling Small Children**)

___ I expect isolation will be a challenge. (Continue below)

I will handle my feelings of isolation by:

___ Scheduling regular get-togethers with friends

___ Attend local networking events

___ Get involved with online peer groups

___ Join Chat sessions

___ Scheduling regular get-togethers with business contacts/clients

___ Other: _____

_____

_____

Handling Small Children

___ I have no small children. (Skip to **Summary**)

___ I will implement the following structure for my children: _____

_____

_____

_____

_____

I will schedule daycare the following day(s)/time(s): _____

_____

_____

_____

Summary

What resources have been helpful and/or what additional information do I need to investigate in order to balance work and home?

_____

_____

_____

_____

_____

_____

_____

_____

_____

_____

_____

Chapter Eight: Ethical Considerations

Accurately Representing Your Experience and Capabilities

I will represent my expertise and capabilities as:_____

_____

_____

I will NOT accept any projects for skills/expertise I do not have, including: _____

_____

_____

_____

These are the tasks I know I'll need to refer to another VA. I've identified these VAs as potential "partners" that have these skills and will work with me to provide support for these types of projects:

Task: _____   Resource VA:_____

Notes: _____

Task: _____   Resource VA:_____

Notes: _____

Task: _____   Resource VA:_____

Notes: _____

Task: _____   Resource VA:_____

Notes: _____

Task: _____   Resource VA:_____

Notes: _____

I will create the following ethical standards for my business and incorporate them into my marketing materials or website:

_____

_____

_____

Keeping Client Files Safe

I will use the following options for keeping client files safe and confidential:

_____

_____

_____

_____

Summary

What resources have I found helpful and/or what additional information do I need to investigate in order to consider the ethics of my business?

_____

_____

_____

_____

_____

_____

_____

_____

_____

Chapter Nine: Growing Your Business

Adding Staff

What options would work best for growing my business?

___ Sub-contractors

How I can find good sub-contractors: _____

_____

_____

What my interview process will be: _____

_____

_____

_____

Create and implement a good sub-contractor agreement. Some of the information I will need in that agreement includes:

_____

_____

_____

_____

How will I communicate projects and work effectively with my subs? _____

_____

_____

_____

_____

What hourly rate will I pay for subs: $ _____ per hour or _____% of my hourly rate.

This will allow me a profit of $ _____ per hour, or _____%

Employees ____

What skills/expertise do my employees need to have? _____

_____

_____

_____

_____

Where will I find prospective employees? _____

_____

_____

What will the interview process be? _____

_____

_____

_____

Will I need a non-compete contract? If so, what should it include? _____

_____

_____

_____

How will I train my employees and communicate client projects? _____

_____

_____

_____

_____

What tax exposure will this employee add to my bottom line? (check with your CPA):

$ _____ for: _____

$ _____ for: _____

$ _____ for: _____

$ _____ for: _____

$ _____ for: _____

$ _____ for: _____

$ _____ for: _____

When you Need to Move Out of Your Home Office

I believe I need leased space to move my business forward because: _____

_____

_____

_____

_____

_____

Leased space options in my area are:

Location: _____

Leased by: _____

Contact Person/info: _____

Length of Lease:_____

Monthly Rental Cost: $ _____

Cost per square foot: $ _____

Repairs/maintenance not covered by lessor: _____

_____

Notes/Viability of this location: _____

_____

_____

_____

Location: _____

Leased by: _____

Contact Person/info: _____

Length of Lease:_____

Monthly Rental Cost: $ _____

Cost per square foot: $ _____

Repairs/maintenance not covered by lessor: _____

_____

_____

Notes/Viability of this location: _____

_____

_____

_____

Location: _____

Leased by: _____

Contact Person/info: _____

Length of Lease:_____

Monthly Rental Cost: $ _____

Cost per square foot: $ _____

Repairs/maintenance not covered by lessor: _____

_____

_____

Notes/Viability of this location: _____

_____

_____

_____

Growing Your Business Through a Niche

I will grow my business by becoming an expert in the following niche:

_____

What additional training/certification will help me to grow my niche? _____

_____

_____

_____

_____

What marketing changes will get me in front of my niche? _____

_____

_____

_____

_____

_____

Becoming a Leader

Growing my business as a speaker, coach or instructor will require the following training/certification:

_____

_____

_____

_____

_____

How will I market myself in this arena? _____

_____

_____

_____

Summary

What resources have been helpful and/or what additional information do I need to investigate in order to grow my business?

_____

_____

_____

_____

_____

_____

_____

_____

_____

Additional Notes and Resources

www.ingramcontent.com/pod-product-compliance
Lightning Source LLC
Chambersburg PA
CBHW051426200326
41520CB00023B/7373